*God's Pathway
to Healing*

DIABETES

BOOKS BY
REGINALD B. CHERRY, M.D.

GOD'S PATHWAY TO HEALING:

Bone Health

Diabetes

Digestion

Heart

Herbs That Heal

The Immune System

Joints and Arthritis

Memory and Mental Acuity

Menopause

Prostate

Vision

Vitamins and Supplements

Dr. Cherry's Little Instruction Book

God's Pathway to Healing

DIABETES

by

Reginald B. Cherry, M.D.

BETHANYHOUSE
Minneapolis, Minnesota

CONTENTS

INTRODUCTION

There is an epidemic silently spreading across America and the world. It is so silent that more than one in three of the 17 million Americans who have the disease do not even realize that they have it, while another one million U.S. citizens over the age of nineteen will develop the disease in the next year.[1] Other statistics indicate that there are 120 to 140 million people worldwide affected by this epidemic and that these numbers will double in the next twenty-five years. This disease, of course, is diabetes.

Newsweek called diabetes the "next great lifestyle disease epidemic to affect the U.S."[2] Diabetes was the sixth leading cause of death in 1999, directly or indirectly killing approximately 450,000 individuals over the age of twenty-five, and accounting for nearly one-fifth of all deaths in the United States that year. The risk of death for individuals with diabetes is roughly twice that of those without the disease, and about 3.6 times greater for those with the disease between the ages of twenty-five and forty-four. In 2002 an estimated $132 billion was spent to treat diabetes, which is approximately one of every ten dollars spent on health care in the United States. Diabetes is also a major factor in cardiovascular disease, strokes, blindness, kidney disease, nervous system disease, and amputations, among other complications. Odds are that we all have at least one friend or family member that has diabetes and/or that we have it ourselves.[3] Personally, I have had several relatives who were diabetic. I thank God that my wife, Linda, and I have normal blood-sugar levels; however, we still take steps to prevent the disease every day.

Such statistics are sobering at best, but often are more likely to cause fear and anxiety. But God has not given us a spirit of fear, but of power, and of love, and of a sound mind. (See 2 Timothy 1:7.) In other words, whether we or one of our loved ones face diabetes, there are things we can do to combine natural wisdom and supernatural faith to heal the disease. God has not left us helpless or alone. He has a pathway to healing diabetes for any who come to Him.

One of the most alarming and, strangely enough, hope-giving facts about diabetes is that it has been linked closely to our modern American lifestyle. The incidence of diabetes was much lower several decades ago. What is it about our modern lifestyle that is contributing to this new prevalence of diabetes? Primarily diet, lack of exercise, and being overweight. Why is this also "hope-giving"? Because by changing certain lifestyle habits and by using the wisdom God has given us as well as new findings by modern medical science, diabetes can be controlled.

Though the medical community still

believes that there is no known cure for diabetes, as Christians we know that "with God all things are possible" (Matthew 19:26; Mark 10:27). Throughout my more than twenty-five years of practice as a doctor of preventive medicine, through the guidance of the Holy Spirit as I have researched medical journals and the Word of God, I believe God has shown me some amazing things to help people find God's pathway to healing for them. It is my hope and prayer that if you are facing diabetes yourself, reading this pocket book will be a first step toward God's pathway to healing diabetes for you or someone you know.

—Reginald B. Cherry, M.D.

Chapter 1

DIABETES: THE SILENT EPIDEMIC

Chapter 1

DIABETES: THE SILENT EPIDEMIC

Be sober, be vigilant; because your
adversary the devil walks about like a
roaring lion, seeking whom he may
devour. (1 Peter 5:8 NKJV)

Be on your guard and be careful that
you are not led astray. (Luke 21:8 AMP)

Keep Satan from getting the advantage
over us; for we are not ignorant of his
wiles and intentions. (2 Corinthians
2:11 AMP)

Because diabetes is a disease that can
creep up on an individual slowly and silently,

it is good for all of us to understand what it is, what causes it, what it does, how to detect it, and how to avoid or treat it. The symptoms can be present for years while the individual either doesn't notice them because they have come on so gradually or because he or she has ignored them. Meanwhile, diabetes does its damage.

With 17 million Americans suffering from diabetes (while 5.9 million do not even know they have it) and one million new cases occurring each year—almost 2,750 new cases a day—it will touch all of us in some way, whether through a family member, a co-worker, a friend, or ourselves. The odds are that one in twenty Americans has diabetes. In addition to this, over 26 million Americans are pre-diabetic, which simply means that they will develop the disease.[1] Other statistics indicate that there are 120 to 140 million diabetics worldwide and that these numbers will double in the next twenty-five years. Cases of diabetes have increased 30 percent in the past eight to ten years overall and roughly 70 percent for individuals in their thirties. In fact, it is estimated that by 2028 as many as one in four Americans will have developed diabetes. Not only because of its prevalence but also because the threat of diabetes more than triples the risk of premature death for younger to middle-aged adults, all of us should do what we can to avoid it and to help others learn how to avoid it as well.

FAMINE IN THE MIDST OF ABUNDANCE

Diabetes mellitus, the most common form of diabetes, is a disease that interferes with the body's ability to metabolize certain nutrients, primarily glucose, the type of sugar our body "burns" to produce energy. The name comes from the Greek and Latin words for *fountain* and *honey* because ancient diagnosticians noticed that sufferers produced large amounts of "sweet" urine that attracted ants. Diabetes mellitus creates this problem by interfering with the function of insulin or the amount being produced. Insulin is the hormone that regulates the metabolism of glucose as well as other carbohydrates, fats, and starches. When the cells become insulin-resistant or the amount of insulin in the system is reduced, the cells begin to starve for energy-generating glucose, even though the level of that sugar is increasing all around them because of the lack of insulin to help burn it. As insulin levels drop, blood sugar levels skyrocket. The glucose that the cells need is often only millimeters away, in abundance but unattainable. It is like the proverbial carrot on a stick—the food is there but just out of reach, so the animal runs faster and faster to try to get it. Diabetes mellitus is literally the starvation of cells in the midst of plenty.

Diabetes insipidus is a much less common form of diabetes and interferes with the kidney's ability to conserve water, causing the patient to urinate more often than normal.

This condition is caused by the reduction of the hormone vasopressin, produced by the pituitary gland, which controls the amount of urine secreted by the kidneys. Though it is the second most common form of diabetes, it only makes up a small percentage of overall diabetes cases. Because of our limited space in this book and for the purpose of our general discussion, we will deal primarily with diabetes mellitus.

Diabetes mellitus (which I will refer to in the rest of this book simply as *diabetes*) is categorized into two types. *Type-1 diabetes* has been traditionally known as *juvenile-onset diabetes* because it first appears in children and young adolescents. It is also known as *insulin-dependent diabetes* because it renders the pancreas unable to produce enough insulin to process glucose effectively, which is remedied with daily injections of insulin. Medical science has no known cure for type-1 diabetes, and although natural remedies cannot cure it, they can help make the body more receptive to the insulin supplied by injections. This form of diabetes makes up 5 to 10 percent of all diabetes mellitus sufferers. It must also be diligently monitored to be controlled. Associated risk factors include genetic predisposition, autoimmune disease, and certain environmental factors. There is also some evidence to suggest that type-1 diabetes may also be related to milk and other dairy products eaten at too young an age.[2]

People with type-1 diabetes must work closely with their doctor, using insulin before contemplating the use of any herb supplement or dietary change. Any changes that make the body more receptive to insulin could throw the system into imbalance if the insulin dosage is not adjusted accordingly. With dietary modifications, diabetics will often need from 30 to 40 percent less insulin, but only a knowledgeable physician can determine such critical changes in the dosage of insulin injections.

Type-2 diabetes, or *non-insulin dependent*

diabetes, has traditionally been called *adult-onset diabetes* because it generally occurs in individuals forty-five years of age or older. However, it is now being detected more frequently in younger adults and even in adolescents and children. It is generally associated with the following:

(1) diets high in sugar and starch, junk foods, refined foods, and foods generally deficient in the nutrients our bodies need;

(2) obesity (about 90 percent of all newly diagnosed type-2 diabetics are overweight); and

(3) inactivity, or lack of exercise.

Aging, race and ethnicity (some races are more susceptible), family history of diabetes, and prior history of gestational diabetes (a form of diabetes diagnosed during pregnancy) are also indicators that the disease may eventually develop.

Type-2 diabetes mellitus commonly

occurs because the cells of the body develop a resistance to insulin, which is often the result of frequent "spikes" or sudden increases and decreases in blood sugar levels because of consuming too many sweets, junk food, or a poor diet in general, which can, in turn, cause a sudden spike in the production of insulin in the system. Insulin is used to control blood sugar levels by carrying it to the cells to be burned. Because of the abundance of insulin, the body's cells begin to decrease their cell receptors that respond to insulin (they don't need as many due to the high amounts of insulin and the lack of a need for energy because of a sedentary lifestyle or being over-weight). In effect, the cells try to reduce their consumption of glucose by rejecting the insulin that brings it to them. This causes yet higher blood sugar levels, which then trigger more insulin to be produced by the beta cells of the pancreas and again results in the cells' decreasing their insulin-responding cell receptors to keep from being overloaded.

Because of this vicious cycle, no matter how much insulin is produced, it—and the glucose it carries—is not entering into the cells properly. Deprived of their prime energy supply, muscle and nerve cell function slowly decrease, which explains why early signs of diabetes are fatigue and irritability.

The body must then also face the problems of high insulin levels in the blood. The higher the level of insulin, the greater the risk of obesity, further accelerating the cycle. This cycle then, unless reversed, spirals on to eventual overload. The cells begin to starve because they have so few insulin-responsive cell receptors; blood sugar levels rise further; and the pancreas, again, produces even more insulin. High insulin levels also attack cell walls, increasing the risks of heart disease and stroke. After a sustained period of high insulin production, the pancreas's ability to manufacture insulin "burns out," and insulin levels drop dramatically. This drop in insulin combined with the insulin intolerance of the cells is what causes the serious complications of diabetes. This final stage of type-2 diabetes can require insulin injections as treatment to keep the patient functioning somewhat normally.

Another interesting risk factor of diabetes, according to a study at the Harvard School of Public Health reported in the *American Journal of Epidemiology,* is, oddly enough, snoring. While snoring is often linked to being overweight, it was considered to be a coincidence; yet when this team did a study factoring weight out of the picture, thin people who were heavy snorers still had twice the risk of diabetes as those who did not snore. It appears that snoring impairs the proper intake of oxygen, which triggers the release of stress-related compounds called *catecholamines,* which, in turn, result in increased resistance to insulin. One of the ways to alleviate this is to see that the patient doesn't sleep on his or her back. This can be done, for example, by nudging the person to get him or her to turn over. You may want to discuss possible solutions with your family physician to seek other methods of prevention. While several surgeries have been designed to relieve snoring, none have shown long-term success. But there may be other causes that your doctor can help you address.

Type-2 diabetes makes up 90 to 95 percent of all diabetes mellitus cases. Despite the dangers of its pervasiveness, it is being shown in test after test to respond well to lifestyle changes and treatment. In other words, there are things that we can do to prevent it and even reverse it. The natural and medical interventions outlined in the rest of this book will primarily address how to control—and hopefully cure—type-2 diabetes mellitus.

What Are the Early Warning Signs of Diabetes?

One of the first symptoms a person will notice in the early stages of diabetes will be that he or she will drink more water (doctors call this *polydipsia*). This is because the body is trying to dilute the high blood sugar levels. That person will then also begin to urinate more frequently because of the greater fluid intake, putting more strain on the kidneys.

The individual may also begin to lose weight because the body's cells are not getting the glucose they need to provide energy. At the same time, the person will be hungry more frequently because his or her body is starving in the midst of plenty; so it tries to take in more and more calories to compensate. This is especially a negative if much of the diet is made up of sugary junk foods, as this will further fuel the destructive diabetes cycle. We will talk more in the next chapter about the type of diet that will reverse the diabetes cycle caused by the spiking blood insulin and sugar levels associated with sugar-laden junk foods.

Brief periods of numbness and tingling—especially in the extremities of the hands and feet—can also be an indicator of developing diabetes, as can bouts of blurring vision. As the metabolism begins to slow because of the starvation of the cells, the person will also begin to experience periods of tiredness, irritability, and lassitude, or lethargy.

If you are experiencing one or more of these symptoms regularly enough to be concerned, it is a good idea to consult with your family physician or health professional to see about testing for diabetes. As with any disease, catching it early will make it easier to treat. There is also reason for comfort if the results to such a test are negative, though you will still want to follow the precautions outlined in the next chapter to keep diabetes from developing later.

HOW DO YOU CHECK FOR DIABETES?

There are a variety of tests for diabetes, many of which function by measuring the amount of glucose in the bloodstream after a night's fasting or giving the patient 75 milligrams of glucose and then checking their blood sugar level two hours later. This latter is called a Glucose Tolerance Test (or GTT). Normal glucose levels range from 70 to 110 milligrams per deciliter of blood. Impaired Fasting Glucose (IFG) is a pre-diabetic condition marked by blood sugar levels between 110 and 125 mg/dL. Impaired Glucose Tolerance (IGT) is another, though more serious, pre-diabetic classification for glucose-tolerance-test blood-sugar levels between 140 and 199 mg/dL. Statistics indicate that one in four Americans has no symptoms of diabetes but already has a developing level of insulin resistance. Those who test to be Impaired Glucose Tolerant—or with a fasting blood sugar level of 126 mg/dL or above—on two separate occasions are considered to be diabetic, as are those who have a one-time glucose tolerance blood sugar level higher than 200 mg/dL. Diabetics can too commonly go higher than 300 mg/dL on these tests.

However, the best test to monitor diabetes is known as the A1C glycosalated hemoglobin test, or hemoglobin A1C test. Because daily sugar levels fluctuate so much, this is a better test. Levels of hemoglobin A1C reflect blood sugar levels over the preceding three months. On this test, to be normal, the score should be *seven* or less.

WHY SHOULD WE BE SO CONCERNED ABOUT DIABETES?[3]

The complications of diabetes are numerous and severe. It can lead to anything from wounds healing more slowly and a higher risk of infections to problems as serious as cardiovascular disease, reduced blood flow, blindness, amputation of limbs, nerve tissue damage, and, worst of all, death due to complications of any of these, or diabetes itself. Many of these complications are the result of the high amount of blood sugar that begins interacting with proteins and then attacking the blood vessels or nerves at the same time as the pancreas is overworked to produce too much insulin, which also attacks the blood vessel walls and arteries, greatly increasing the risks of heart attack and stroke. Understanding these problems can give us a better respect for the disease as well as more specific things to pray about for those we know who suffer from it.

CARDIOVASCULAR PROBLEMS

Heart disease is the leading cause of death among adults with diabetes and causes death about two to four times more often in diabetics than in their peers without diabetes. Heart attacks kill 75 percent of those with diabetes. Roughly 73 percent of adults with diabetes have high blood pressure (hypertension) or use prescription medications to keep their blood pressure under control.

STROKE

The risk of having a stroke is two to four times greater for diabetics.

BLINDNESS

Diabetic retinopathy causes 12,000 to 24,000 new cases of blindness every year and is among the leading causes of blindness. The root cause of this disease is the decreased flow of oxygen caused by high glucose levels in the blood, which also leads to blockage in the blood flow to the retinas. The eyes attempt to remedy this by forming new blood vessels and capillaries in the retinas, which are often very fragile and tend to break and leak, causing scar tissue and clouding or blurring vision. Diabetics also have an increased risk of developing cataracts. Diabetes is the leading cause of new blindness among those between twenty and seventy-four years of age. While laser therapy can be used to treat these complications, there are also natural remedies for this that we will discuss in chapter 3.

KIDNEY DISEASE

Diabetes is also the leading cause of treated end-stage renal disease, causing 43 percent of new cases each year. In 1999 alone, 38,160 diabetics began treatment for end-stage renal disease and 114,478 underwent dialysis or kidney transplant, which is roughly half of all who received these treatments for kidney disease. Diabetes causes this condition because it damages the small blood vessels that feed the kidneys, cutting off nutrition and oxygen to the kidneys while at the same time increasing the kidneys' work in their effort to filter out the high blood sugar levels. It is painfully ironic that the kidneys literally burn out trying to flush out the very food that they need. Diabetics who smoke have an even further increased risk of kidney damage.[4]

NERVOUS SYSTEM DISEASE

Somewhere between 60 and 70 percent of those with diabetes have nervous system damage, or neuropathy, resulting in numbness, loss of feeling, or pain in their hands or feet, slowed digestion of food in their stomachs, carpal tunnel syndrome, impotence, and/or other nerve-related problems. *Diabetic neuropathy* is the most common complication of diabetes. Once diabetes develops, the blood vessels begin to clog, obstructing the flow to the smaller vessels and capillaries that feed the nerves, causing a 50 percent reduction in the flow of vital nutrients and oxygen. This is what causes the numbness, tingling, and loss of feeling in the feet and hands that is an indicator of diabetes. Nerve damage due to diabetes, known as peripheral neuropathy, can also cause ulcers that result in the amputation of arms and legs.

Another common complication of diabetes that affects the nervous system is *autonomic neuropathy*. This generally affects the digestive system, slowing down the function of the intestines and often causing the stomach to empty improperly because of the backup of food. Food and its nutrients will remain in the stomach and not exit out into the body because the nerve endings that tell the body the food is there have been deadened. This condition can also lead to impotence if it affects the nerve endings in the genital area.

AMPUTATIONS

Because of the reduced blood flow and deterioration of nerves and other cells, diabetes causes more than 60 percent of all non-accident-related amputations in the United States. There were, on average, about 82,000 nontraumatic lower limb amputations due to diabetes each year in the United States between 1997 and 1999. That is approximately 225 a day, or more than one every seven minutes!

DENTAL DISEASE

Periodontal or gum disease is more common in those with diabetes. Young adult diabetics are often at twice the risk of their peers. Almost one-third of diabetics have severe periodontal disease with the loss of five millimeters or more of the attachment of the gums to the teeth.

COMPLICATIONS IN PREGNANCY

Poorly monitored or poorly controlled diabetes before conception and during the first trimester causes major birth defects in 10 to 15 percent of pregnancies, and miscarriages in 15 to 20 percent. In the second and third trimesters, it can result in excessively large babies that can pose a risk to both mothers and infants.

Another complication that can occur in pregnancy is the development of gestational diabetes, a form of glucose intolerance that can develop in the expectant mother. It is most common among African-Americans, Hispanic/Latino Americans, and Native Americans, as well as those with a family history of diabetes. Roughly 5 to 10 percent of women who develop gestational diabetes during pregnancy will have type-2 diabetes after the pregnancy, and 20 to 50 percent of the rest of them will develop diabetes in the next five to ten years.

OTHER COMPLICATIONS

Uncontrolled diabetes can cause a number of biochemical imbalances that can lead to such conditions as diabetic ketoacidosis or hyperosmolar (nonketotic) comas, which are life-threatening. Because of the decreased energy available to the body, diabetes also significantly impairs the immune system, making the patient more susceptible to other illnesses, and once those illnesses are acquired, they are often more severe and harder to overcome. Diabetics are much more likely to die from influenza or pneumonia than those without the disease.

THE REAL DANGER IS IGNORING THE PROBLEM

The good news is that, for most of us, diabetes is preventable and treatable. Proverbs tells us, "The complacency of fools will destroy them" (Proverbs 1:32 NIV). In dealing with diabetes, medical doctors find complacency to be the biggest problem. People think diabetes won't strike them; then they begin to notice that they are more thirsty than usual and they need to urinate more frequently, or they have a little blurred vision that comes and goes. They have some numbness in their foot or hand and ignore it. All the while diabetes is beginning to do its damage, and they are plodding along without acknowledging that they have a medical challenge that could kill them.

I certainly don't tell you all of this to scare you, but I do want to get your attention. We cannot afford to ignore diabetes and hope it will go away; we must do something about it. Whether we have the disease or not, there are things we can do to avoid it or to keep it from becoming a detriment to the full, abundant life God has promised us in His Word (see Psalm 91:16 and John 10:10). We should not be ignorant of the wiles of this enemy who is set against us. We need to understand how diabetes works so that we can better understand how to address it. Understanding of the disease is the foundation on which we can build its defeat.

In John 9, Jesus healed a blind man by mixing His saliva with some soil, placing it on the man's eyes, and telling him to go wash it off in the pool of Siloam. Now, I believe that Jesus could have healed this man in a number of different ways, including a simple command that the man's eyes be opened and then going on His way, but I also believe that Jesus did it this way at this time to teach us something. He took a natural element (soil), combined it with something of himself (saliva), and then left the man with something to do (wash in the pool of Siloam) in order to finish his own healing. The man could have washed his face somewhere else; we have no indication that the pool of Siloam was the closest source of water. Yet when the man obeyed the instructions Jesus gave him, he was healed. Just as Naaman had to wash himself seven times in the Jordan to receive his supernatural healing (see 2 Kings 5:1–14), there was something this blind man had to do for himself in order to see again.

I believe that God's pathway to healing for many of us follows this same pattern: First, we take something natural, or that medical science has determined will be helpful, we combine it with supernatural faith and the presence of God in our lives, and then we follow the instructions given to us to facilitate our healing. By combining the best wisdom medical science has to offer with the divine guidance of the Holy Spirit in our lives, God can work the healing miracle that we need, whatever it might be. I urge you to read this book carefully and prayerfully, as well as to see your personal physician to discuss the health concerns you may have regarding diabetes. Then follow God's plan for your health as His Spirit leads you. God has promised health and healing in His Word to those who will follow and obey Him. We simply need to act on whatever He tells us. His part is the healing; our part is searching out His wisdom and obeying it.

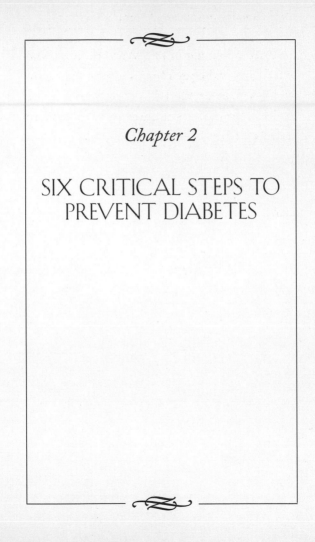

Chapter 2

SIX CRITICAL STEPS TO PREVENT DIABETES

Chapter 2

SIX CRITICAL STEPS TO PREVENT DIABETES

There will be mighty and violent earth-
quakes, and in various places famines
and *pestilences (plagues: malignant and
contagious or infectious epidemic diseases
which are deadly and devastating);* and
there will be sights of terror and great
signs from heaven. (Luke 21:11 AMP,
italics added)

In this passage, Jesus spoke of devastating
and epidemic diseases that we would face in
the last days. We can certainly consider diabetes to be in this category as we look at the

astounding statistics about its spread and the severity of its complications. However, Jesus also told us in this same passage, "Be on your guard and be careful that you are not led astray" (Luke 21:8 AMP) and "Not a hair of your head will perish. By standing firm you will gain life" (Luke 21:18–19 NIV). God has a plan for how we can successfully face all of the challenges of our time—we simply have to plug into His Spirit to receive His instructions and then follow His guidance to the letter.

To this end, I would like to share with you six things that you can do to prevent diabetes before it develops in your life as well as how to control it if this disease has already struck you. If you have already tested diabetic on either the GTT or A1C test, then you will want to couple the lifestyle changes in this chapter with some of the more short-term treatments outlined in the next chapter. However, since improper nutrition, lack of exercise, and being overweight are three of the leading causes of diabetes, it is a good idea to get these under control at the same time as you take medications to directly address the symptoms of diabetes that lead to the adverse complications of the disease. The six areas we should pay attention to in order to prevent diabetes are the following:

1. Minerals
2. Antioxidants
3. Essential Fatty Acids
4. Diet
5. Exercise
6. Weight Management

These are not in any order of importance, nor are they steps that have to be taken in any specific order. In fact, for best results, they should all be implemented at the same time. To better understand each of these, we will discuss them in more detail in the following sections.[1]

1. MINERALS

Because of the depletion of our soils and factory farming methods for harvesting our meats, foods are being depleted of their vital nutrients, particularly of their mineral content. One study shows that many of the vegetables we eat today are anywhere from 10 to 81 percent lower in vital minerals than they were in the 1930s. The result has been that the general U.S. population is also deficient in these minerals. To compensate for this, we need to know how much of each mineral we should be getting regularly, and either eat more foods that contain them or begin a solid nutritional supplement program that includes all of them. (For more information on nutritional supplements and what should be included in them, please visit our Web site at *www.abundantnutrition.com*, the resource section at the end of this book, or my pocket book entitled *God's Pathway to Healing: Vitamins and Supplements.*)

CHROMIUM. This mineral is one of the most critical nutrients for maintaining proper insulin levels, which in turn control blood sugar levels (decreasing the need for the pancreas to overproduce insulin) and help the cells get the glucose they need to burn for energy. All of these work together to keep the threat of diabetes far from us.

Recent studies also show that as many as 80 percent of Americans have suboptimal levels of this crucial element in their daily diets. Most diets contain less than 30 micrograms of chromium daily, while 200 micrograms is the recommended daily minimum. My wife, Linda, and I take a supplement that safely gives us 300 micrograms of chromium picolinate and nicotinate a day, which is the level I recommend as a preventative.

The food that is highest in chromium is brewers' yeast, but it is difficult to get enough of this into our diets to get the chromium we need. You can also get chromium from nuts, broccoli, mushrooms, prunes, and asparagus, among other fruits and vegetables. I normally recommend taking it in supplement form, as this is the easiest and most reliable way to maintain constant levels of any vitamin, mineral, or other nutrient in our bodies, though it is also good to back up such supplementation with more of these foods in our regular diet. Since our foods overall are depleted of this trace element, getting too much is not nearly as great a concern as not getting enough, and the more sources we get it from, the better.

VANADIUM. This mineral has an insulin-like effect, helping to promote normal insulin function by "driving" glucose into the cells, and thus also decreasing fasting blood sugar levels. Personally, Linda and I take 300 micrograms of vanadium a day in our daily supplement support program.

MAGNESIUM. This mineral affects several different body systems, including nerve function, heart rhythms, and energy metabolism, and it increases insulin sensitivity and the uptake of glucose into the cells. Grains are typically high in this mineral, though it is also easily taken in supplement form. It is deficient in approximately 60 percent of the overall American population. I recommend taking 400 milligrams of magnesium a day.

ZINC. Seventy-five percent of us do not get enough zinc, and many of these are diabetics. Zinc is also very effective in controlling blood sugar levels. I recommend 15 milligrams a day of zinc as both a preventative and treatment for diabetes.

2. ANTIOXIDANTS

High glucose levels cause increased "oxidative stress," which gives free radicals free rein to tear up the cells and linings of our bodies. As you may know, free radicals are "renegade" oxygen molecules that have lost an electron and so search our systems for an electron from somewhere else. When they find one, they throw the molecule the electron is taken from into imbalance and change its structure. These "torn" or altered molecules then become problems for cells and often turn them cancerous. Within blood veins they cause tears in the linings, which can trigger blood to begin to clot just as a cut in our skin triggers blood to clot to keep us from bleeding to death. This damage heightens the complications of diabetes, many of which are also caused by reduced blood flow.

Antioxidants act by finding these free radicals before they do damage and "latch onto them" by giving them the electron they need; then they either escort them out of our system or release them as normal oxygen cells to be absorbed beneficially by our system. By cleaning up these free radicals, antioxidants keep our system more balanced, make useful oxygen more plentiful, keep blood flow strong to supply nutrients and oxygen to all of our organs and muscles, and reduce the chances of illness and the effects of aging.

Because of these multiple benefits, I suggest taking antioxidants regularly within your supplement program. The crucial ones are vitamin C (2,000 milligrams per day); vitamin E (800 IU per day); alpha lipoic acid (ALA) (50 milligrams per day); beta carotene (20,000 IU per day); and selenium (200 micrograms per day).

3. ESSENTIAL FATTY ACIDS

There are certain "good fats" that our bodies need to stay healthy and strong, and primary among these are the omega 3 fatty acids found in most cold water fish, such as salmon, herring, trout, and sardines. The main two of these are eicosapentaenoic acid and docosahexaenoic acid, which are more commonly referred to by their initials: EPA and DHA.

These omega-3 fatty acids have been shown in several studies to improve glucose tolerance. EPA and DHA are also fundamental building blocks for our nervous system cells and nerve sheaths. I recommend 360 milligrams of EPA and 240 milligrams of DHA daily. These are most easily taken in gel capsule form to maximize absorption and to keep a constant level of these critical fatty acids in our system at all times.

4. DIET

The foods we eat are critical to preventing diabetes. When we look at a lifestyle change as major as changing our diets, though, it is important to have a framework rather than just a list of do's and don'ts. This is why I have long been a proponent of the Mediterranean diet, as it is perhaps the healthiest in the world. This may be why the new food pyramid suggested by some Harvard doctors looks very much like the typical meal plans found in the Mediterranean region.[2]

If you have read any of my other books

(particularly *The Bible Cure*), you will already know something of the Mediterranean diet. However, for those of you who have not, I will take the time to discuss it in some detail here. It is a diet that is low in red meats, hydrogenated oils, and processed foods (major sources of bad fats and cholesterols), and high in fiber, nuts, fish, fruits, vegetables (especially in salads), and olive oil (sources of good fats and cholesterols and other nutrients our bodies need)—all of which are also mentioned in the Bible and are the staples of dishes from Israel, Greece, Italy, and other nations that surround the Mediterranean Sea. Fat, especially cooked fats, and salt reduction are both very important for diabetics. Recent studies also show that as little as two servings daily of whole grain foods and fiber can decrease the risk of diabetes by as much as 33 percent.

If you were to take a look at menus from Mediterranean countries, you would see that the following items make up most of what is eaten there every day:

1. **Olive oil.** Olive oil replaces most fats, oils, butter, and margarine. Extra-virgin olive oil is preferred over other varieties.

2. **Cinnamon.** Though this is only one of various spices used in Mediterranean cooking, cinnamon has been shown by USDA studies to significantly increase insulin activity.

3. **Breads.** Dark, chewy, high-fiber crusty bread is present at most meals in the Mediterranean. Another good choice is Ezekiel bread, a recipe based on Ezekiel 4:9. (Typical American white bread made from processed white flours is not part of this diet.)

4. **Pasta, rice, couscous, bulgur, potatoes.** Pasta is often served with fresh vegetables and herbs sautéed in olive oil; occasionally it is served with small quantities of lean beef. Tomato sauces that are often served with pasta are high in lyco-

pene, one of the most potent antioxidants. Brown rice is preferred. Couscous and bulgur are other forms of whole grains.

5. **Grains.** To get healthy grains from many different sources, eat cereals containing wheat bran (one-half cup, four to five times a week), or alternate with cereals such as Bran Buds (one-half cup) or those containing oat bran (one-third cup). According to a study cited in a recent issue of the *American Journal of Clinical Nutrition,* eating whole grains such as brown rice, oats, corn, and barley, is protective against type-2 diabetes. In another study on whole grains, Teresa Fung of Simmons College in Boston and her colleagues looked at the eating and lifestyle habits of nearly 43,000 healthy men over a twelve-year period. The results showed that the men who consumed the least amount of whole grains (a little under half a serving per day)

were nearly 60 percent more likely to develop type-2 diabetes than men who consumed more whole grains (more than three servings per day). Apparently, whole grains contain vitamins and nutrients that may be important in reducing the risk of this disease. (Refined grains—those found in cookies, doughnuts, white pasta, and white rice—on the other hand, lack vitamins and nutrients. Also, refined grains more than double the amount of sugar in the blood and cause more insulin to be secreted than whole-grain products.) Bran Buds, in particular, is a great diabetes fighter, because it contains psyllium, a water-soluble fiber that can reduce blood sugar levels by 11 percent during the day and can lower post-meal glucose levels by up to 20 percent. Oat bran also reduces blood sugar levels, as it has a fiber in it that is in the same family as psyllium. Grains, especially oat bran and oatmeal, are also high in magnesium, which is also key to stabilizing blood sugar levels. Eating these with soy milk rather than regular milk adds extra benefits because soy is a whole protein (for more information on soy, see the next subsection).

6. **Fruits.** Several different fruits are available in the Mediterranean area, and they are usually eaten raw at least two or three times a day. Bananas, in particular, are not only high in potassium, but studies also have shown that two bananas a day can lower blood pressure up to 10 percent, which is both one of the complications of diabetes and one of the factors contributing to other damage caused by diabetes. Prunes are also high in chromium, which is key to proper insulin function. You should eat five prunes a day to get their full benefit.

7. **Beans.** You should include various kinds of beans in your diet: pinto, great northern, navy, lentils, kidney, etc. Bean and

lentil soups are very popular in the Mediterranean countries and are usually prepared with a small amount of olive oil. You should have about one-half cup of beans three or four times per week. In one study performed by the University of Kentucky, type-1 diabetics who consumed one-half to one cup of beans daily decreased their insulin dosage by 38 percent, and most of the type-2 diabetics who did the same were able to stop insulin injections all together. Substances in common beans increase the insulin receptor sites of body cells and thus reverse the trend that generally causes type-2 diabetes.

8. **Nuts.** Eating ten raw unsalted almonds or walnuts a day has some wonderful benefits. Almonds, in particular, are higher in dietary fiber than most nuts, and have the essential diabetes-fighting mineral, chromium. Macadamia nuts and peanuts also appear to have some

benefits for diabetics, though they should be limited in number because of their high fat content.

9. **Vegetables and herbs.** Dark green vegetables are prominent in the Mediterranean diet, especially in salads. The updated food pyramid that has recently been appearing in science and news magazines suggests that vegetables should be eaten daily "in abundance." I suggest eating at least one of the following cruciferous vegetables daily: cabbage, broccoli, cauliflower, turnip greens, or mustard greens; and at least one from the following group of fruits and vegetables daily: carrots, spinach, sweet potatoes, cantaloupe, peaches, or apricots. Raw onions have a compound known as *diphenylamine,* which is very similar to the prescription diabetes medication Tolbutamide and can therefore reduce blood sugar levels. Onions also contain quercetin, which has been shown to reduce the

risk of retinal damage associated with diabetes. More and more studies are also showing that the equivalent of one clove of garlic a day (an herb used widely in the Mediterranean) can protect against free radicals and reduce blood pressure as well as counter the tendency of blood to clot. Asparagus and mushrooms are great sources of chromium.

10. **Yogurt.** Eating fat-free live-culture yogurt daily has some incredible benefits. The live bacteria in yogurt (lacto bacillus, streptococcus, and acidophilus) significantly strengthen the immune system, which is good for all of our body systems as well as those specifically attacked by diabetes (freezing yogurt to make it a dessert kills these good bacteria). A light breakfast of one cup of fat-free yogurt sprinkled with ten almonds and chopped fruit is a great start to the day. Drinking six ounces of Concord grape or orange juice, which is some-

thing my wife and I do every morning, also has tremendous benefits. Eating yogurt with your morning nutritional supplements can reduce the "vitamin taste" that often lingers after taking tablets and capsules alone. Another low-fat breakfast alternative would be oatmeal or bran flakes with soy milk and fruit. Either of these is a healthy alternative to the more traditional breakfast of sausages, eggs, pancakes or French toast, or sugary cereals with whole milk.

11. **Cheeses.** Mediterranean countries tend to eat lighter-colored dairy or white goat cheeses, usually grated or broken up on salads or in small wedges combined with fruit for a dessert. Unlike other milk products, recent studies indicate that cheese might not contribute to clogged arteries as much as was previously believed. Still, it is wise to eat reduced- or low-fat cheeses (fat-free cheeses are often rubbery and not very palatable).

While all of these should be eaten daily, meats and proteins, on the other hand, should be eaten only a few times a week or month. I would put these in the following order of frequency and importance:

1. **Fish.** Cold-water fish high in omega–3 fatty acids such as cod, salmon, mackerel, and herring; trout is also good. As you will remember from the previous section, these essential fatty acids are very beneficial for insulin function and help protect our nervous system from damage. Fish is the healthiest meat we can have in our diet. A Dutch study showed that people who ate fish were half as likely to develop diabetes as those who didn't.

2. **Poultry.** White breast meat without the skin is best. Poultry can be eaten two or three times a week.

3. **Eggs.** Eggs should be eaten no more than two or three times a week. Even fewer is better.

4. **Red meat.** The fat in red meat is the

least desirable kind of fat. When God spoke in Leviticus about avoiding fat, I believe this is the type of fat He was referring to. The fat and cholesterol from red meat are the main contributors to the fatty plaque that can plug our arteries or create the sudden blockages that cause heart attacks or strokes, which are leading killers of diabetics. Red meat eaten in Mediterranean countries tends to be much leaner and is eaten only two or three times a month. If you do include red meat in a meal, be sure to eat small portions of leaner cuts and trim off whatever fat you can before you cook it.

While the Mediterranean diet is not an absolute for diabetes prevention, it does give what I consider to be the best and easiest outline to follow for what we should eat to keep our system healthy. While changing our diet is probably one of the more difficult on this list of six things to do, it is also one of the most beneficial.

SOYBEANS: THE PLANT KINGDOM'S BEST PROTEIN SUBSTITUTE

While the soybean is not necessarily a part of the Mediterranean diet, it has several beneficial characteristics that make it worth mentioning here. First of all, it is an excellent protein substitute for red meat. You can receive whole proteins from the plant kingdom by combining certain vegetables (beans and rice or corn, for example), but it appears that soy is the only plant that is a complete protein in and of itself. In other words, it is the only plant that has all of the essential amino acids necessary for the formation of proteins in one package.

Soy is now available in a variety of products, including tofu, tempeh, soy ice cream, milk, yogurt, cheese, flour, and even roasted soy nuts. Tofu is perhaps the most popular form. Having no real flavor of its own, tofu absorbs flavor from whatever it is cooked with. It can easily be worked into a wide variety of recipes to suit people with all sorts of tastes. I must admit that my wife and I have not been able to add tofu to our diets because of the texture. However, I would encourage you to at least try it for yourself. (But I can definitely understand if you choose another way to get the benefits of soy!)

The way we have worked around this is to drink soy milk. We regularly have it on our breakfast cereal. We started with vanilla soy milk and have found a variety of others that we like, including chocolate and "creamy" (this is not mixed with cream but thickened with other natural proteins).

5. EXERCISE

Exercise can lower blood sugar and decrease body weight if done regularly, but it also directly fights diabetes by increasing the need for energy consumption in cells, which, in turn, increases the number of insulin cell receptors. In one study, those who exercised five or more times weekly had less than half the cases of diabetes as a similar group who exercised less than once a week. Those exercising two to four times a week had a 38 percent lower incidence of diabetes when compared with the low exercise group. Even those who exercised only once a week had a 23 percent lower incidence of the disease than the group with slightly less exercise.

When I talk about regular exercise, I am referring to something as simple as walking forty to forty-five minutes, three to five times a week; or you can break it down further to a brisk walk every day for about twenty minutes. This is enough to get your heart rate up and doesn't require an expensive membership to a health club. Obviously you could do more (it is even advisable to start with less if you find this too challenging), but I have always believed in starting with simple changes and then working your way up as God leads you. It is also important not to start with too much activity, since that can stress your system more than help. Any activity you add to your lifestyle will help, but a brisk walk of three miles in forty-five minutes three to four times a week is all that is needed to do wonders in preventing diabetes.

Walking, jogging, stationary cycling, outdoor cycling, water exercise, tennis, stretching, aerobic exercise, and swimming are also all fine workouts. The important thing is to find something you enjoy and can do regularly that builds the aerobic capacity of your heart, lungs, and other body systems, forcing the cells to demand more energy, which will raise your metabolism and keep blood sugar lower. As you improve your fitness, you can combine various forms of exercise to address all your different muscle groups and body systems for a fuller life all around. Being fit and trim has benefits all its own for overall self-esteem and quality of life. Remember to do proper warm-ups and cool-downs. It is also better to eat after exercising rather than before as this will contribute to maximized food absorption and calorie burning.

DETERMINE YOUR SAFE HEART-RATE RANGE

Whatever exercise you choose, work at it vigorously enough to get your heart rate elevated during the time you are exercising. Physical fitness experts have a simple formula for determining a safe heart-rate range for exercising. Simply subtract your age from 220 to find your maximum heart rate. If you are 40 years old, your formula would be 220−40=180. Your target heart-rate zone is between 60 and 80 percent of that number. So multiply your maximum heart rate by 0.6 for the bottom of your safe exercise range and by 0.8 for the top. As you exercise, check your pulse rate now and then to be sure your heartbeat is within that range. The safe heart-rate range for a forty-year-old would be 108 to 144.

Find your pulse in your wrist or neck, count the number of heartbeats in ten seconds, and multiply that number by six. If the number you get is within your safe exercise range, you're fine. If it's lower, work harder.

If it's higher, slow down a little. When starting an exercise program, aim at the lowest part of your target zone for the first few weeks. Gradually build up to the higher part of your target zone.

6. WEIGHT MANAGEMENT

Being overweight (obesity is defined as being thirty or more pounds overweight) is a leading contributor to the development of type-2 diabetes mellitus. Not surprisingly, 60 to 70 percent of Americans are overweight. Getting down to your proper weight by eating the right foods and exercising addresses all of the greatest contributors to diabetes at once! I put weight management last on the list because if you do the other five this one will usually take care of itself. Most of our patients who have had the greatest success and longest term weight loss have combined following the Mediterranean diet with a regular exercise program. In a study of 3,234 people who tested pre-diabetic, those who lost from 5 to 7 percent of their body weight and moderately exercised thirty minutes a day reduced their risk of developing type-2 diabetes by 58 percent.[3]

Because of this and the long-term health risks involved in many of the most popular weight-loss diets on the market today, I recommend this program of following the Mediterranean diet, plus exercise, over any others. It may take longer on this diet to get down to your optimal weight, and following this plan is not a quick fix that you can do for a bit and then return to the former pattern of eating that caused you to put on the weight in the first place, but lifestyle changes such as this greatly increase the likelihood that you will live the long, full life God has planned for you. In my mind, this benefit far outweighs all the difficulties in making these changes.

DIABETES CAN BE DEFEATED!

These six things should be some of the first steps taken by anyone concerned with diabetes, whether he or she has the disease or not (which includes all of us). One of the great things about these lifestyle changes is that they are not only critical in preventing and controlling diabetes but also greatly help us to prevent other major problems, such as cardiovascular disease, cancer, nervous system deterioration, and many other health challenges. When going on the type of program I recommend for patients, cholesterol levels typically drop 25 to 30 percent, blood pressure drops 10 percent, and people tend to lose weight. God has kept it quite simple for us: Follow the principles of His health and diet laws in His Word and He will keep sickness from the midst of us.

However, our God is not only a God of prevention, He is also a God of healing. I do believe that it is most important that we understand how to keep from developing disease in the first place (I practiced preventive medicine before we started this ministry), but we also need to know that God has a path-

way to healing for us if we are already suffering from the disease. We need to be aware of
what God has revealed to medical science
both in pharmaceutical medications and natural alternatives so that we can let His Spirit
guide us down the pathway to healing that is
right for us. For this reason we will look into
ways of treating diabetes in the next chapter.
My prayer is that through consultation with
your doctor and the leadership of the Holy
Spirit, God will show you the information
that is right for you.

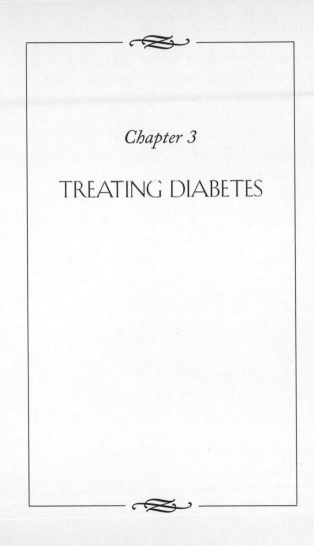

Chapter 3

TREATING DIABETES

Chapter 3

TREATING DIABETES

While preventing diabetes is most criti-cal, what if we already have a fasting blood sugar level above 126 mg/dL and need to address it more directly? While all of the steps to prevent diabetes also work to control it, the higher our blood sugar level is, the more immediate is our need to take steps to get it under control. Knowing it takes some time to alleviate diabetes, we can ill afford to let our blood sugar levels remain too high for too long waiting for lifestyle changes to take effect. As long as diabetes and high blood sugar levels are present, damage is being done, and some of that damage is irreparable or may require surgeries that we would rather avoid. The best solution in such cases is to do what is necessary in the short term to get blood sugar levels back into a normal range, and then to ease off of such interventions when changes in lifestyle begin to bring things back into the proper range. By combining the best of medical science with the wisdom of God, we can get both the best short- and long-term solutions available to us.

Because of this, I am not averse to suggesting prescription medications as a short-term solution for those directly facing diabetes. These medications drop blood sugar levels more quickly than natural alternatives. However, we should still have wisdom about them. We need to understand what the prescription medications are and what they do. Some are better than others and have fewer adverse side effects. Some should not be taken with other medications or natural compounds. We will also want to find the best combinations of prescription medications and more natural treatments so that we can be on the prescription meds for as short a time as possible. For these reasons, as with anything else, we should make our decision about what to take prayerfully, getting the best information possible from our own personal physician and other reliable sources so that God can lead us down the pathway to healing that is best for each of us.

THE BEST PRESCRIPTION MEDICATIONS FOR DIABETES

One of the classic prescription medications for diabetes is a class of trade drugs called Glucotrol. These cause the pancreas to produce more insulin, which is the same short-term solution to insulin resistance that our bodies attempt. While we would like to get insulin levels back to normal long term, we cannot do so without the energy production that insulin causes in the short term, and it is better to get it from the pancreas than through injections. However, though this is still widely prescribed, it is better to use drugs that reduce insulin resistance and help the body to use insulin more effectively rather than increase the amount of insulin in the bloodstream, which, if you remember from chapter 1, is one of the things that contributes to diabetes in the first place, as well as leading to other problems, such as hardening of the arteries, heart attack, stroke, and obesity.

So if the pancreas is still producing insulin, which it is in most type-2 diabetes mellitus cases, then we should look for other treatments rather than furthering diabetes progression by producing more insulin. One of the ways to do this is by addressing the cells' sensitivity to insulin rather than blindly producing more through other interventions. The medicines Glucophage, Avandia, and Actos are some of the best in this class. Each of these works in its own way to reduce insulin resistance and to help the cells use insulin more effectively to burn the excess glucose in our bloodstream (the other problem caused by diabetes). These are all fairly new medications and are not prescribed by many doctors yet, so discussing them as a prescription to treat your diabetes may be suggesting something new to your physician.

Another class of drugs used to treat diabetes is one that slows the breakdown of carbohydrates in the intestines, which helps reduce the spikes in the sugar levels that cause the elevated insulin production. Thus, the absorption of carbohydrates and sugars is slowed to a more gradual and natural rate, and some of the carbohydrates and sugars are passed out of the system before they are absorbed. Either way, spikes are less severe. Two of the best medications in this class are Precose and Glyset.

At this writing, there are as many as twenty other new pharmaceutical medications being tested as treatments for diabetes, which again shows the magnitude of the epidemic growth of the disease and the concern it is causing in the medical community. For more up-to-date information on whether some of these new drugs might be helpful for you, check out our Web site at *www.drcherry.org,* sign up for our monthly newsletter, and then check regularly with your family physician for more information on updates and breakthroughs in the area of diabetes treatment.

VITAMINS, MINERALS, AND OTHER NATURAL SUPPLEMENTS THAT ADDRESS DIABETES

Whether you have been on one of these prescription medications to treat your diabetes for years or have just learned you have the disease and are starting treatment, it is a good time to begin taking natural supplements that can eventually reduce your dependence on these prescription drugs. We all prefer natural remedies, if possible, because they often have few side effects. In the case of diabetes, you will want to try the preventive lifestyle changes prescribed in the previous chapter, but if you are on prescription drugs as well, there are natural compounds you can take that will help you get off of these expensive medications more quickly. Many of these natural compounds act in the same way as the prescription drugs, so when you begin intervention with both, you may soon see a reduction in the dosages of the pharmaceuticals— eventually, of course, you may be able to be off of them altogether. I have actually taken many patients off of prescription medications as they have taken more natural alternatives.

CHROMIUM. This trace mineral is at the top of the list for natural remedies. Chromium actually increases the effectiveness of insulin while decreasing insulin levels. It helps the cells get the glucose they need to get the energy they require to stay strong and healthy. Chromium also lowers fasting glucose levels, which lowers insulin production, and thus also lowers the other risks associated with high blood sugar and insulin levels.

Diabetics also tend to excrete more chromium than most people, further worsening this problem. If you are diabetic, I recommend that you get from 800 to 1,000 micrograms daily as a treatment strategy. Normally I suggest taking two dosages of 500 micrograms a day—one in the morning and one in the evening.

VANADIUM. This mineral is second only to chromium for treating diabetes because of its insulin-like effects. I recommend, and I take, 300 micrograms of this a day, which is the amount I suggest for both prevention and treatment.

BIOTIN. This member of the B-vitamin complex family assists in the metabolism of carbohydrates (it acts like Precose and Glyset, which were discussed in the previous section) and blood sugar within the cells, and increases insulin sensitivity. I recommend 300 micrograms of it daily both as a treatment and preventative.

NIACIN. This vitamin B_3 component increases carbohydrate metabolism. There has been some controversy about using niacin to treat diabetes, but small amounts of it have been shown not to have detrimental effects on blood sugar levels. I suggest 100 milligrams of niacin a day as part of your daily nutritional supplement program.

MAGNESIUM. This mineral is commonly deficient in diabetics as well as approximately 60 percent of the overall American population. Because of the multiple benefits of it to all the systems of the body, but especially to controlling blood sugar and insulin levels, I recommend 400 milligrams per day.

ZINC. I recommend 15 milligrams a day of zinc as both a preventative and treatment for diabetes.

ESSENTIAL OMEGA-3 FATTY ACIDS. As we

discussed in the previous chapter, EPA and DHA improve glucose tolerance but also help to repair the nerve abnormalities that are so common in diabetics, since they are also fundamental building blocks for our nervous system cells and nerve sheaths. I recommend 360 milligrams of EPA and 240 milligrams of DHA daily for both the prevention and the treatment of diabetes.

HERBAL COMPOUNDS THAT CAN HELP DEFEAT DIABETES

Along with certain vitamins and nutritional supplements that you can take to help defeat diabetes, there are also a few herbs that help in treating the disease. These extracts may also be effective in preventing some of the complications that are caused by diabetes.

GYMNEMA SYLVESTRE. This bushy plant that grows in India is probably the most common herb mentioned in medical literature as a treatment for diabetes and has been used in this way for thousands of years. In one study, 400 milligrams of a gymnema extract was given to twenty-seven type-1 or insulin-dependent diabetics. After ten to twelve months, the participants were managing their blood glucose so much better that many of them were able to lower their requirements for insulin injections. In another study, twenty-two type-2 or non-insulin-dependent diabetics were also given 400 milligrams of a gymnema extract. Over the next eighteen to twenty months, the participants experienced significant decreases in both blood glucose levels and hemoglobin A1C levels. These improvements allowed many in the study to decrease their intake of blood-sugar-lowering drugs, and five of the twenty-two were able to discontinue their medications altogether. Another study using a dosage of 400 milligrams of gymnema showed that it dropped blood sugar on an average from 232 mg/dL to 152 mg/dL.

From certain animal tests, it also appears

gymnema may help regenerate beta cells, which are the cells of the pancreas that produce insulin and which type-2 diabetes wears out in its vicious cycle of forcing more and more insulin production as cells become more and more insulin-resistant. This is truly astounding because there is no other known substance that can regenerate pancreatic cells after they have ceased to function. More tests are needed to verify that this compound has the same effect on humans, but the evidence is very promising.

This herb is generally available without a prescription from most health food stores or as part of our blood sugar support program that you can access online at *www.abundantnutrition.com* (for further information on this, please see the "Resources Available From Reginald B. Cherry Ministries, Inc." at the back of the book). Because of the research results, I recommend a daily dosage of 400 milligrams of gymnema sylvestre to treat diabetes.

BITTER MELON. This herb, also known as mordica, contains a molecule that is similar to insulin. It is called a polypeptide, or P-type insulin. It is a common shrublike plant that grows in India, Asia, Africa, and South America. Studies show this herb increases the glucose uptake by body cells and thus lowers blood sugar levels. A common recommendation is 100 to 200 milligrams of this extract three times a day to treat diabetes.

FENUGREEK. The part of this plant that is extracted to treat diabetes is the fibrous portion of its seed. Fenugreek contains six different ingredients that help regulate blood sugar. It works by absorbing carbohydrates in the intestines and thus lowers the amount of glucose produced to be spread through the system. It also increases good HDL cholesterol levels, so it has the additional benefit of protecting against heart disease. The recommended dosage is 15 to 25 grams of extract per day.

BILBERRY. Tests have shown that extracts

from this cousin of the blueberry decrease blood sugar levels by as much as 26 percent and the blood fat triglycerides by up to 39 percent (which is also commonly high in diabetics). This compound also protects the blood vessels in the back of the retina and thus prevents the retina damage or cataracts that are too commonly associated with diabetes. I recommend 100 milligrams of this daily, though it can also be taken safely in higher dosages.

SILYMARIN. This herb is the active compound in milk thistle and is more commonly associated with the treatment of liver disease and hepatitis C. It has been shown in studies to decrease fasting blood sugar levels as well as A1C levels.

ALOE VERA. The journal *Phyto-Medicine* reported several significant studies about the effectiveness of aloe vera in regulating blood sugar levels. One study found a significant drop—from an average of 250 mg/dL down to 141 mg/dL—of fasting blood sugar levels in people regularly taking aloe vera extract alone.

GLUCOMANNAN AND ABSORBALEAN. Both of these fiber supplements are readily available at most health food stores. Fiber, especially water-soluble fiber, is very helpful for diabetics because it absorbs carbohydrates before they are turned into sugar and thus limits the amount of sugar that ends up in the bloodstream.

Glucomannan comes from the root of the konjac plant that grows in Japan. It is very impressive in its ability to bind, or tie up, sugars in the gastrointestinal tract before they can be absorbed into the bloodstream. AbsorbaLean is a blend of ten different fiber extracts that are concentrated and put into capsule form so that it can easily be added to a daily nutritional supplement program.

NATURAL TREATMENTS FOR SOME OF THE COMPLICATIONS OF DIABETES

Because some of the more common complications of diabetes are as dangerous, if not more so, as the disease itself, I thought it would also be good to dedicate some space in this book to discussing some natural treatments that will more directly help prevent these problems. You will find some duplication between these compounds and those on previous lists. Because of the possible adverse side effects of taking too much of some things, do not add the two amounts together for the same compound but rather take the larger of the two recommended dosages. For example, if you want to take bilberry for both its benefits in defeating diabetes and its help in keeping your eyes healthy, take just 25 milligrams of it a day rather than doubling that amount to 50 milligrams a day, unless directed otherwise by your personal physician.

TREATING NERVE DAMAGE

Remember that nerve damage occurs in roughly 60 percent of diabetics and the effects of this range from simple numbness and loss of feeling to impotence, poor digestion, and lower limb amputations. Because of its prevalence, it is important for all diabetics to take action to counteract this damage.

ALPHA LIPOIC ACID. Studies have shown that this potent antioxidant, commonly abbreviated ALA, can reduce the high blood sugar levels that clog circulation and cause nerve damage by around 20 percent. It does this by improving the metabolism, or breakdown, of sugar in the muscle cells, also increasing the amount of energy available to the individual, and has the added benefit of protecting against cataracts. It also helps to regenerate other important antioxidants—Vitamins C and E—in the body. For diabetics who have neuropathy, I recommend 600 to 800 milligrams of ALA a day. However, my wife and I take 50 milligrams of this in our daily supplements as a preventative.

GAMMA LINOLENIC ACID. GLA is found in evening primrose oil, flaxseed oil, and borage oil. I suggest 360 to 400 milligrams of it daily because of its tremendous help as a treatment for neuropathy. I also recommend a daily dosage of 90 milligrams of GLA for everyone as a preventative. Many advanced daily nutritional supplement programs now have this or a similar amount of GLA as a regular component.

INOSITOL. This nutrient, which is a B-vitamin, is vital for proper insulin function, which, of course, helps to control blood sugar levels and reduces the clogging that causes neuropathy. I recommend taking 50 milligrams of this extract daily for diabetics.

B-VITAMINS. A good B-complex vitamin has great benefits for treating nerve damage. Seventy to 90 percent of Americans get less than the recommended daily allowances of these vital B-vitamins. Tests have shown that 80 percent of those with neuropathy notice some benefit from vitamin B_1. Thus, taking a good B-complex is a great recommendation for all of us. I recommend taking one that has 50 milligrams of B_1, 50 milligrams of B_5, 75 milligrams of B_6, and 100 milligrams of B_{12} every day.

TREATING EYE PROBLEMS

As we discussed before, diabetic retinopathy is one of the leading causes of blindness. Though laser surgery can greatly benefit those suffering from this complication, I strongly recommend trying these more natural treatments.

VITAMINS B_6, C, AND E. Seventy-five milligrams of vitamin B_6 daily has a great benefit for numerous biochemical pathways of the body, including alleviating the problems in the capillaries of the retina that cause diabetic retinopathy. The antioxidant vitamins C and E reduce the damage free radicals can do in the eyes as well as the rest of the body. I recommend 2,000 milligrams of vitamin C and 800 IU of the natural form of vitamin E every day.

Large dosages of vitamin E supplements may be useful in treating type-1 diabetes as well as have benefits for type-2 diabetics, according to Massachusetts researchers Dr. George King of Joslin Diabetics Center of Boston and his colleagues, in their article in *Diabetics Care,* "Oral Vitamin E Treatment Appears to Be Effective in Normalizing Retinal Blood Abnormalities and Improving Kidney Function." In this clinical trial, subjects had taken vitamin E for only four months. The researchers also noted that at the end of the study period, retinal blood flow had increased to near normal rates, and kidney function had also improved.

BILBERRY. We have already discussed the benefits of this extract for both diabetes and eye care in a previous section. Again, I recommend 25 milligrams of it daily.

MAGNESIUM. Because this mineral is so important in lowering blood glucose levels that can clog small blood vessels and capillaries, which greatly helps reduce retina damage, and because of the general deficiency of it in the American population, I recommend 400 milligrams of magnesium a day for everyone. (Please see the section above entitled "Vitamins, Minerals, and Other Natural Supplements That Address Diabetes" for more information on the benefits of magnesium.)

QUERCETIN AND HESPERIDIN. Twenty-five milligrams of these two bioflavonoids daily will help reduce the risk of cataracts that can be common in diabetics.

TREATING KIDNEY PROBLEMS

Another major complication that diabetics face is kidney damage. Over half of those requiring dialysis because of end-stage kidney disease are diabetic as well. The following nutrients have tremendous benefits for helping the kidneys stay healthy.

B-VITAMINS. The same problems of high blood sugar levels that cause retinal and nerve damage also cause kidney damage because the high blood sugar levels block the capillaries that feed the kidneys in addition to over-working the kidneys as they try to filter the sugar out of the system. Because of this, B-vitamins are also crucial to proper kidney function. B-vitamins also lower homocysteine levels (high homocysteine levels contribute to clogging of the vessels, so lowering this level in the blood helps blood flow, reduces kidney damage, helps alleviate cardiovascular disease, and helps many other organs in the body). For these benefits, I again suggest a balanced B-complex that includes folic acid, B_6, and B_{12} in dosages comparable to what we have discussed in previous sections.

ALPHA LIPOIC ACID. As with the B-vita-mins, because of the benefits ALA has to blood flow, I recommend it to help the kidneys as well. I would advise 600 to 800 milligrams of ALA a day for diabetics and 50 milligrams of this a day for everyone else.

GRAPE-SEED AND GRAPE-SKIN EX-

TRACTS. These extracts have the wonderful benefit of reducing the capillary ruptures that contribute to kidney disease. I recommend 50 milligrams a day of grape-seed extract and 25 milligrams a day of grape-skin extract. These extracts are also available in many balanced daily nutritional supplement programs.

FROM DIABETES TO WHOLENESS

As we have already discussed, the onset of diabetes is not a death sentence, although it can be if ignored. Because of its epidemic rise, we all need to do what we can to avoid its effects for both ourselves and our loved ones. By making the lifestyle changes discussed in the previous chapter and adding to that the medications and natural interventions outlined in this chapter when you need to more directly address diabetes, the disease can be controlled and perhaps eliminated as a threat to our fullness of life as we grow older.

Again, I urge you to apply the principles

of John 9 to find your unique pathway to healing. By combining natural and spiritual wisdom with prayer, and consultation with your personal doctor, God will lead you to do that which is right for you. In the previous chapters we have discussed much of the natural and medical wisdom you will need for this journey; in the following chapter we will discuss steps to getting God's guidance for the correct pathway to healing for you. But please remember, knowing what to do is only part of the solution. Once you learn what to do, you have to discipline yourself to follow those instructions every day. If you ask Him and seek His face, God will show you the way to your healing; then pray that He will also help you develop the self-control and diligence to make those solutions part of your lifestyle so that you can live in the abundance He has for all of us until the end of our days.

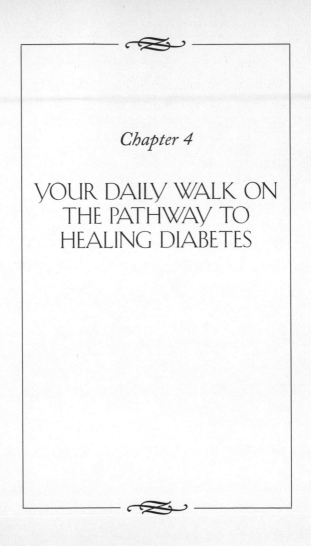

Chapter 4

YOUR DAILY WALK ON THE PATHWAY TO HEALING DIABETES

Chapter 4

YOUR DAILY WALK ON THE PATHWAY TO HEALING DIABETES

Ye shall serve the LORD your God, and he shall bless thy bread, and thy water; and *I will take sickness away from the midst of thee*. There shall nothing cast their young, nor be barren, in thy land: *the number of thy days I will fulfill*. (Exodus 23:25–26, italics added)

This passage of Scripture has always been a central one to our ministry. God so clearly links His blessings of health to our bread and water, symbolic of the things we eat and drink. This seems especially relevant to our discussion of diabetes because its cure is also dependent on our diet.

Notice that God also ties the blessing to service to Him. I have always believed that serving God is not ministry alone—as many people immediately assume when they hear the words "serving God"—but in walking in His guidance in everyday life. Certainly we serve Him by following His instructions to us in our churches, but we also serve Him by obeying His words to us in conducting ourselves in our places of employment, in nurturing our families, in our social lives, and in taking care of ourselves. As the Scriptures say,

> Don't you know that you yourselves [your bodies] are God's temple and that God's Spirit lives in you? If anyone destroys God's temple [your bodies], God will destroy him; for God's temple is sacred, and you [your bodies] are that temple. (1 Corinthians 3:16–17 NIV, bracketed words are author's)

God clearly wants us to take care of ourselves

so that we can live long lives as lights for Him on this earth.

I believe we also see in this the pattern of how God wants us to operate in our lives: by combining spiritual principles with natural wisdom, or more specifically in this example, combining God's laws and blessing with our diet, we direct our health and our service to Him. Because of this, I have five steps to take toward developing this combination of spiritual and physical well-being in our lives. They outline how we can find either His plan for healthy living (if we are maintaining our health and avoiding disease) or His pathway to healing whatever health challenges we or our loved ones may be facing.

Step 1: Consult with a physician or reliable medical professional. Make sure you have regular checkups to catch potential problems early when they are easiest to treat and correct. Many say that they don't need to go to doctors because they are doing all the things they should be doing in order to maintain their health. I believe we need to do both: live healthy lifestyles and see our doctors regularly. One need not exclude the other. As I have said before, regular checkups are often the only opportunity to catch health problems while they are still simple to treat. Having a healthy checkup can also keep you from unnecessary worry about your health. Regular checkups also give you the chance to discuss with your doctor your plans for maintaining, or regaining, your health.

Consultation with a physician or a competent medical professional actually gives you something very important that books such as this cannot—insight into solutions or maintenance plans that specifically fit your unique medical and physical needs. Be sure to discuss with your health advisor all the various compounds and/or medications you are taking to ensure that there are no conflicts. This person may even be able to suggest a packaged supplement program that contains all or most of what you need on a daily basis. Also discuss your diet and exercise programs to see if he or she has any other advice that might be helpful to you in these areas. This first step is crucial to finding the pathway that is unique for you or for a loved one for whom you are responsible.

Step 2: Pray with understanding. Seek God in prayer and ask Him to reveal to you and to your doctor the best natural steps you can take to proceed down your pathway to maintaining health or receiving healing.

While much of the advice I have offered in this small book is practical for the body, do not neglect your daily spiritual needs. Make sure to "supplement" the information you take in to your mind and body every day with solid doses of God's Word and prayer—also avoiding those things that are harmful to your spirit in the same way that you avoid junk foods or other things that are harmful to your "temple." Only then can God lead you into the fullness and abundance of life He has promised in all areas.

If you are not sure how to pray for diabetes, you can begin by praying a prayer like
the following one for yourself or your loved
ones, changing it as the Spirit of God leads
you, in order to make it fit the specific concerns and needs you want to address:

*Father, I thank you in the name of Jesus that
you have an answer to the curse of diabetes.*

*Father, strengthen the beta cells in my kid-
neys so that they can continue to produce the
normal levels of insulin that I need. Lord, please
also increase the insulin receptors in my cells to
reverse insulin resistance, lower my blood sugar
levels, and help my cells get the energy they need
to be strong and healthy. Please keep my blood
flow strong and remove blockages in my vessels
and arteries so that the nutrients and oxygen my
cells need will reach all the different parts of my
body in the amounts needed, even to the extremities of my fingers and toes, the smallest capillaries in my eyes and kidneys, as well as all of my
other organs, muscles, and nerve cells. I also pray*

that you will help lower my fasting blood sugar to 126 mg/dL or below and that my A1C level will be below seven. I trust in your healing power and believe the lifestyle changes I make and the compounds I take are the result of your leading me on the pathway to healing you have uniquely designed for me.

Quicken to me things I should do to change my lifestyle and eating habits to protect my body against the complications of diabetes. Help me to cultivate the fruit of self-control to make these habits part of my normal routine. Guide me as I develop a daily nutritional supplement program so that I get the nutrients I need most to remain a strong and healthy light for you in everything I do. Please also reveal to me the medications or natural alternatives that are best for me to defeat diabetes. I pray that your healing anointing will flow through these substances, and that if I need to take pharmaceutical medications, that it will be for as short a time as possible as more natural compounds take their place. However you lead me, I will be obedient to the guidance of your Holy Spirit.

Thank you, Father, for setting me free from sickness and disease as you bless what I eat and drink, and that I will fulfill the number of my days according to your promises.

In Jesus' name I pray. Amen.

Step 3: Ask the Holy Spirit to guide you to truth. I have given you a great deal of information about things you can do or take to help your physical body control and defeat diabetes, and it is quite possible that your medical advisor will give you some other options. By referring to the information in this book, you can bring up the discussion of what would be best specifically for you. Approach your health professional by asking if he or she would be willing to work with you in developing a diet, exercise program, or nutritional supplement program, or can suggest other steps for you to take to keep diabetes from being a threat to you or your loved ones.

I strongly encourage you to explore all the aspects of the information I have shared with you in this book. Pray in faith that God will give you the wisdom you need in order to discern the pathway to healing that is best for you. In James 1:5 we have God's promise about receiving this wisdom: "If any of you lack wisdom, let him ask of God, that giveth to all men liberally, and upbraideth not; and it shall be given him." Jesus also told us, "But when he, the Spirit of truth [the Holy Spirit], comes, he will guide you into all truth" (John 16:13 NIV, bracketed words are author's). Allow the Holy Spirit to guide you to *all* truth, including the proper care of your physical body.

Step 4: Maintain proper and healthy nutrition. Exercise your body and mind to stay fit. In other words, dedicate yourself to living the diabetes-defeating lifestyle outlined in chapter 2. Make these things a regular part of your routine and remember to make them fun as well and not a burden. Find a variety of foods and recipes that you like that are typical of the Mediterranean diet and experiment with these healthy natural ingredients to create your own delicious meals. Find an exercise program you enjoy—while some may like walking on a treadmill while watching television, others will need to get outside or find a competitive sport to challenge them or a group activity, such as dance or stretching classes, to encourage them socially as well. Don't let it become drudgery or you won't keep it up over time.

Studies have shown that we also need to challenge ourselves intellectually to maintain healthier mental faculties. Find things to do to exercise your mind as well: playing games, writing your memoirs for your family, or studying things you have always wondered about. Establish an active life for an active body and mind.

Step 5: Stand firm in God's pathway to healing for you. Refuse to be discouraged or defeated. Be aggressive in prayer and in faith, claiming your health and healing in Jesus Christ. And when God shows you through a reliable source how to make a lifestyle change, put it into action.

GOD HAS A UNIQUE PATHWAY TO HEALTH FOR YOU

There are nineteen individually recorded healings in the Gospels, and each is unique in its own way. I believe these are all recorded in the Scriptures to show us that God uses different pathways to manifest His healing power. When I realized this, it totally changed the way I practiced medicine. In fact, when I started praying and asking God to show *me*, as a doctor, His pathway to healing for each of my patients, I began to see more clearly His design for helping each person. Through prayer, faith, knowledge, and wisdom, God can show you His pathway to maintaining health or to receiving healing.

If we are open to this knowledge and

wisdom, God will work miracles. It may be instantaneous, or it may be a process or treatment that takes some time. Just as many chronic diseases such as diabetes or cardiovascular disease take time to develop, they will also take time to be reversed. Our healing may involve certain prescription medications for a time or even surgery. Or it may be a pathway that is uneventful as we maintain our health through regular checkups. Thank God that we can pray for our healing, and also that we can take precautions before we are sick to avoid the need for healing. Either way, as Christians we have tremendous hope.

Hebrews 11:1 says that faith gives substance to those things hoped for. If you don't have anything to hope for, how will faith give substance to it? You have to have hope, and that hope comes when you know that God has a pathway to health or healing for you. That is a promise you can cling to, pray for, and have faith in. Thank God for His promises!

These are principles you can apply in all areas of your life, but you can specifically apply them with regard to your physical health. Seek God in the areas where you have particular health concerns and receive His answers. See a physician to get specific information that will guide you in your prayers. God knows your needs and also the best way for you to receive your healing and maintain your health. Hold on to the hope of His promises, and He will show you His plan for healthy living that is especially designed for you.

ENDNOTES

Introduction

1. American Diabetes Association, "National Diabetes Fact Sheet." Online at: *www.diabetes.org/main/info/facts/facts_natl.jsp.* Accessed: 22 May 2003.
2. Jerry Adler and Claudia Kalb, "An American Epidemic: Diabetes" *Newsweek* (4 September 2000).
3. ADA, "National Diabetes Fact Sheet."

Chapter 1

1. ADA, "National Diabetes Fact Sheet."
2. Healthwell.com, "Diabetes: Part 2: Dietary and Lifestyle Changes." Online at: *www.healthwell.com/healthnotes/Concern/Diabetes.cfm#Life-Options*. Last updated: 2 August 1999. Accessed: 29 May 2003.
3. Many of the statistics in this section were

taken from the ADA's "National Diabetes Fact Sheet."

4. Healthwell.com, "Diabetes: Part 2: Dietary and Lifestyle Changes."

Chapter 2

1. It should be noted that many of the compounds in this chapter are also discussed in the following chapter, though dosages in this chapter are for prevention, while dosages in chapter 3 are for treatment. Do not add these two numbers together if you want to both begin to prevent *and* treat diabetes, but rather take the higher dosage recommended in chapter 3.

2. For more information on the new food pyramid, see Walter C. Willet, P. J. Skerrett, and Edward L. Giovannucci, *Eat, Drink, and Be Healthy: The Harvard Medical School Guide to Healthy Eating* (Simon & Schuster, 2001).

3. This study was cited in Rita Elkins, M.H. "Defending Against Diabetes," *GreatLife* (March 2002): 22.

REGINALD B. CHERRY, M.D.—A MEDICAL DOCTOR'S TESTIMONY

The first six years of my life were lived in the dusty rural town of Mansfield, in the Ouachita Mountains of western Arkansas. In those childhood years, I had one seemingly impossible dream—to become a doctor.

Through God's grace, I graduated from Baylor University and the University of Texas Medical School. Throughout those years, I felt God tug on my heart a number of times, especially through Billy Graham as I heard him preach on television. But I never surrendered my life to Jesus Christ.

In those early days of practicing medicine, I met Dr. Kenneth Cooper and became trained in the field of preventive medicine. In the midseventies I moved to Houston and established a medical practice for preventive medicine. At that time, I am sad to say, money became a driving force in my life.

Nevertheless, God was good to me. He brought into our clinic a nurse who became a Spirit-filled Christian, and she began praying for me. In fact, she had her whole church praying for me!

In my search for fulfillment and meaning in life, I called out to God one night in November 1979 and prayed, "Jesus, I give you everything I own. I'm sorry for the life I've lived. I want to live for you the rest of my days; I give you my life." A doctor had been born again. And by the way, that beautiful nurse, Linda, who had prayed for me and shared Jesus with me, is now my wife.

Not only did Jesus transform my life but He also transformed my medical practice. God spoke to me and said, "I want you to establish a Christian clinic. From now on when you practice medicine, you will be *ministering* to patients." I began to pray for patients who were seeking God's pathway to healing in the supernatural realm as well as in the natural realm.

Over the years we have witnessed how God has miraculously used both supernatural and natural means to heal our patients and to demonstrate His marvelous healing and saving power.

I know what God has done in my life, and I know what God has done in the lives of our patients. He can do the same in your life. He has a unique pathway to healing for you! He is the Lord that heals you (see Exodus 15:26), and by His stripes you were healed (see Isaiah 53:5).

Linda and I are standing with you as you seek God's pathway to healing or preventing diabetes in your life.

If you do not know Jesus Christ as your personal Lord and Savior, I invite you to pray this prayer and ask Jesus into your life:

Lord Jesus, I invite you into my life as my Lord and Savior. I repent of my past sins; I ask you to forgive me. Thank you for shedding your blood on the cross to cleanse me from my sin and to heal me. I receive your gift of everlasting life and surrender all to you. Thank you, Jesus, for saving me. Amen.

ABOUT THE AUTHOR

Reginald B. Cherry, M.D., did his pre-med at Baylor University, graduated from the University of Texas Medical School, and has practiced diagnostic and preventive medicine for more than twenty-five years. His work in medicine has been recognized and honored by the city of Houston and by President George W. Bush when he was governor of Texas.

Dr. Cherry and his wife, Linda, a clinical nurse who has worked with Dr. Cherry and his patients during the past two-and-a-half decades, now host the popular television program *The Doctor and the Word,* which has a potential viewing audience of 90 million homes weekly. They also publish a monthly medical newsletter and produce topical audiocassette teachings, pocket books, and booklets. Dr. Cherry is author of the bestselling books *The Doctor and the Word, The Bible Cure,* and *Healing Prayer.*

RESOURCES AVAILABLE FROM REGINALD B. CHERRY MINISTRIES, INC.

Books

Prayers That Heal: Faith-Building Prayers When You Need a Miracle

Combining the wisdom of over twenty-five years of medical practice and the revelation of God's Word, Dr. Cherry provides the knowledge you need to pray effectively against diabetes, cancer, heart disease, eye problems, hypoglycemia, and fifteen other common afflictions that rob you of your health.

Healing Prayer

A fascinating in-depth look at a vital link

between spiritual and physical healing. Dr. Cherry presents actual case histories of people healed through prayer, plus the latest information on herbs, vitamins, and supplements that promote vibrant health. This is sound information you will need to keep yourself healthy—mind, soul, and body.

God's Pathway to Healing: Bone Health

Bone mass loss and osteoporosis affect more than 34 million Americans today, and statistics indicate that these numbers will continue to grow dramatically in the decades to come. Though bone disease affects four times the number of women as men, the men who suffer from its complications are often twice as likely to die from them as are women. None of us has room to ignore this debilitating ailment; we all need to do what we can now to either prevent or reverse its effects. In this pocket book, Dr. Cherry shares with readers the things they can do, no matter their age, to strengthen bones and immensely reduce the risk of bone mass loss, which results in fractures that can rob us of the quality of life God promised us, if not take life from us altogether. This is a book for all ages and both sexes, as building strong bones is an issue all of us need to address.

God's Pathway to Healing: Digestion

Dr. Cherry discusses keys to a naturally healthy digestive system, including better digestion and absorption of food, proper elimination of waste, and the place of "good" bacteria. He points readers toward better eating habits and natural nutritional supplements to improve digestion.

God's Pathway to Healing: Heart

Heart disease kills twice as many people as all the various forms of cancer combined, and more than half of the body of Christ dies of coronary artery or cardiovascular diseases. However, there are things that you can do to remain free of heart disease. An incredible wealth of research in recent years has been done on natural extracts and foods that will feed this life-sustaining muscle and keep it strong and healthy. When these nutrients are combined with faith, prayer, and God's Word, you will find yourself on God's pathway to healing and a healthy heart.

God's Pathway to Healing: Herbs That Heal

Learn the truth about common herbal remedies and discover the possible side effects of each. Discover which herbs can help treat symptoms of insomnia, arthritis, heart problems, asthma, and many other conditions. Read this book and see if herbs are part of God's pathway to healing for you.

God's Pathway to Healing: The Immune System

We are truly fearfully and wonderfully made, and part of that amazing creation is something God built into us to keep us all healthy for life: our immune system. In this insightful pocket book, Dr. Cherry explains the basic function of this "everyday miracle," which even medical science has yet to fully understand, as well as steps we can take to keep it strong and balanced so that it will do what God designed it to do: "take sickness away from the midst of thee" (Exodus 23:25).

God's Pathway to Healing: Joints and Arthritis

Painful joints and arthritis do not have to be part of aging, Dr. Cherry says. Recent medical breakthroughs show that natural substances can relieve pain and inflammation and slow or prevent cartilage loss.

God's Pathway to Healing: Memory and Mental Acuity

As the baby-boomer generation ages, we are facing more problems with mental function than ever before. Whether it is because of age-related memory loss or poor nutrition or pollutants in the air that affect the way we think or concentrate, people of all ages need new information about how to keep their minds healthy and strong. In this pocket book, Dr. Cherry addresses these concerns in an easy-to-understand and straightforward manner that can help people who are facing ailments such as depression, attention-deficit hyperactivity disorder (ADHD), migraine headaches, Alzheimer's disease, and other concerns that we associate with the brain's function. This pocket book may well be God's key for you to a healthy memory and a sharp, focused mind.

God's Pathway to Healing: Menopause

This pocket book is full of helpful advice for women who are going through what can be a very stressful time of life—menopause. Find out which foods, supplements, and steps lead to a pathway to healing and relief for menopause and peri-menopause.

God's Pathway to Healing: Prostate

This pocket book is packed with enlightening insights for men who are searching for ways to prevent prostate cancer or those who have actually been diagnosed with this disease. Discover how foods, plant-derived natural supplements, and a change in diet can be incorporated into your life to help you find a pathway to healing for prostate disease.

God's Pathway to Healing: Vision

Macular degeneration, cataracts, vision degeneration due to complications of diabetes, and other eye conditions can be slowed or prevented. Dr. Cherry discusses herbs and nutritional changes people can make to keep their vision strong.

God's Pathway to Healing: Vitamins and Supplements

With the huge number of supplements and multivitamins on the market today, it is often difficult to know what to take to get what you need and what not to take to make sure you don't get amounts that might be harmful. This easy-to-follow pocket book is a tremendous reference for anyone who wants to stay healthy in an age when new and epidemic diseases seem to be discovered more regularly than ever before. This pocket book could well be the key to discovering the miraculous power God has unlocked through natural extracts and nutritional supplements to keep His people healthy and whole to the end of their days.

Dr. Cherry's Little Instruction Book for Health and Healing

This book contains easy-to-read information about healthy habits, natural remedies, and nutritional guidance, along with biblical principles for supernatural healing. Also included are prayers and Scripture as a reminder that God's desire is that His people be healthy. This is a helpful volume for readers familiar with Dr. Cherry's work and a great introduction for those who are new to his ministry.

The Bible Cure (now in paperback)

Dr. Cherry presents ancient dietary health laws taken from Scripture. He shows how Jesus anointed with natural substances to heal and how we can activate faith through prayer for health and healing. This book validates scientific medical research by showing God's original health plan.

The Doctor and the Word (now in paperback)

Dr. Cherry explains how God has a pathway to healing for you. Jesus healed both instantaneously and supernaturally, but other healings involved a process. Discover how the manifestation of your healing can come about by seeking His will and His ways.

Dr. Cherry's Study Guides, Volume 2 (a bound volume)

Receive thirty valuable resource study guides from topics Dr. Cherry has taught on the Trinity Broadcasting Network (TBN) program *The Doctor and the Word*.

OTHER HELPS

Basic Nutrient Support

Dr. Cherry has developed a daily nutrient supplement that is the simplest to take and yet the most complete supplement available today. Protect your body daily with over sixty natural substances that fight cancer, heart disease, and many other problems. Call Natural Alternatives at (800) 339–5952 to place your order. Please mention service code "BN30" when ordering. (Or order through the company's Web site: *www.Abundant Nutrition.com.*)

Blood Sugar Support

After twenty-five years of clinical experience helping people maintain healthy blood sugar levels, Dr. Cherry has developed the **Blood Sugar Program**. A key component of this program is **Solumet**,™ a carbohydrate blocker. This slows the absorption of sugar into the bloodstream and also helps maintain normal cholesterol and triglyceride levels.

The second vital part of the program is **Blood Sugar Support**—an advanced blend of nutrients and herbs that have been proven in clinical studies to help balance and maintain healthy blood sugar levels.

God has given us the wisdom and the

tools we need to take a Pathway to Healing.

Call Natural Alternatives at (800) 339-5952 to place your order. Please mention service code "BN30" when ordering.

Reginald B. Cherry Ministries, Inc.
P.O. Box 27711
Houston, TX 77227-7711
1-888-DRCHERRY

BECOME A PATHWAY TO HEALING PARTNER

We invite you to become a pathway partner. We ask you to stand with us in prayer and financial support as we provide new programs, resources, books, pocket books, and a one-of-a-kind monthly newsletter.

Our monthly Pathway to Healing Partner Newsletter sorts through the confusion about health and healing. In it, Dr. Cherry shares sensible biblical and medical steps you can take to get well. Every issue points you to your pathway to healing. Writing from a Christian physician's Bible-based point of view, Dr. Cherry talks about nutrition and health, how to pray for specific diseases, gives updates on the latest medical research, shares Linda's own recipes for healthy eating, and includes questions and answers concerning issues you need to know about.

In addition, we'll provide you with Dr. Cherry and Linda's ministry calendar, broadcast schedule, resources for better living, and special monthly offers.

This newsletter is available to you as you partner with the Cherrys through prayer and monthly financial support to help expand this God-given ministry. Call or write us to find out how you can receive this valuable information.

Become a pathway partner today by writing:

Reginald B. Cherry Ministries, Inc.
P.O. Box 27711
Houston, TX 77227-7711
Visit our Web site:
www.drcherry.org
1–888-DRCHERRY